D0729792

Living the
Ten Commandments
as a Catholic Today

Living the 10 Commandments as a Catholic Today

**Compiled and Edited by
Mathew Kessler, C.Ss.R.**

Liguori
LIGUORI, MISSOURI

Imprimi Potest: Thomas D. Picton, C.Ss.R.
Provincial, Denver Province, The Redemptorists

Published by Liguori Publications, Liguori, Missouri
To order, call 800-325-9521 or visit www.liguori.org.

Library of Congress Cataloging-in-Publication Data

Living the Ten commandments as a Catholic today / compiled and edited by Mathew Kessler.—1st ed.
    p. cm.
   "The articles that comprise this book were written by experts in Scripture or moral theology and appeared in *Liguorian* magazine in 2007 and 2008"—Introd.
   ISBN 978-0-7648-1849-3
   1. Ten commandments--Criticism, interpretation, etc. 2. Catholic Church—Christian authors. 3. Christian ethics—Catholic authors. I. Kessler, Mathew J.

   BV4655.L557 2009
   241.5'2--dc22

                                2009010222

Liguori Publications, a nonprofit corporation, is an apostolate of the Redemptorists. To learn more about the Redemptorists, visit Redemptorists.com.

Printed in the United States of America
13 12 11 10 09 5 4 3 2 1
First edition

Table of Contents

Contributors

Dianne Bergant, CSA ("What God Has Joined, Let No One Separate: Living the Sixth Commandment"), is a professor of biblical studies at Catholic Theological Union in Chicago, Illinois. She is the Old Testament book reviewer of *The Bible Today* and is on the editorial board of *Biblical Theology Bulletin* and *Chicago Studies.*

Raphael Gallagher, C.Ss.R. ("Promoting a Community of Trust and Justice: Living the Seventh Commandment"), is a Redemptorist priest of the Province of Dublin, Ireland. He is presently an invited professor at the Alphonsianum Higher Institute of Moral Theology in Rome, Italy.

Timothy E. O'Connell, PhD ("Rest, Worship, and Community: Living the Third Commandment") is associate provost for faculty affairs at Loyola University in Chicago, Illinois, where he is also professor of Christian ethics. He is the author of *What Does the Church Teach About Social Justice?* and *What Does the Church Teach About Voting?* (Liguori Publications) and *Making Disciples: A Handbook of Christian Moral Formation* (Crossroad Publishing).

Kevin J. O'Neil, C.Ss.R. ("Swept Up by Love: Living the First Commandment" and "Respect for Life: Living the Fifth Commandment"), is an associate professor of moral theology at Washington Theological Union in Washington, DC. He is co-author of *The Essential Moral Handbook* (Liguori Publications).

Stephen T. Rehrauer, C.Ss.R. ("Living Up to the Name of God: The Second Commandment" and "To Tell the Truth: Living the Eighth Commandment"), is a professor of moral theology in Rome. He is the author of *Theology for Today's Catholic: A Handbook* (Liguori Publications).

Paul J. Wadell, PhD ("Thou Shalt Not Be Unhappy: Living the Ninth and Tenth Commandments"), is professor of religious studies at St. Norbert College in De Pere, Wisconsin. His most recent book is *Happiness and the Christian Moral Life: An Introduction to Christian Ethics* (Rowman & Littlefield).

Mara Kelly-Zukowski, PhD ("Fathers and Mothers, Sons and Daughters: Living the Fourth Commandment"), is professor and chair of religious studies at Felician College, New Jersey.

Introduction

Like Diogenes' relentless search for the honest man, the quest for the meaning of life runs through world literature. In fiction, biography, memoir, and other types of literature, writers have pursued this truth, presuming that if there is an answer, men and women want to know it—and if it can be known, it can be practiced. As the reasoning goes, once people understand the meaning of life, they will be happy. Christians are no exception. Comfortable with their faith, they first look to their tradition, and within that tradition, their own literature, particularly the Bible. The Bible does say something about living a good life, and for several millennia, Christians have looked to the Ten Commandments to provide the way. But as they're stated in two forms (see Exodus 20:1–17; Deuteronomy 5:6–21), the Ten Commandments don't translate into our culture today without some assistance. First it's helpful to recall some biblical history.

Born out of the experience of slavery and liberation, the ancestors of Jesus believed themselves to be the Chosen People. Yahweh had heard their cry and sent Moses to deliver the message to Pharaoh. This is the same God who chose Abraham and Sarah as the beginning of something new, a new people. The covenant God made with them and their descendants was in the form of a conditional offer: "…if you obey my voice and keep my covenant, you shall be my treasured possession out of all the peoples" (Exodus 19:5). Just what that offer meant in terms of testing their commitment and returning to true worship of Yahweh and to care of the poor is much of the content of the Old Testament. Guided by the Law and the Prophets, they would experience the rise and fall of the Davidic kingdom and the deportation of a segment of the population, and foreign oppressors would occupy their land.

In their need to interpret the question, "What does it mean to be God's people at this time?" they looked to their past and those key moments when Yahweh was present to them. One such moment was the conferring of the Ten Commandments (known as the "Decalogue") on Mount Sinai or Mount Horeb, depending on which book of the Bible is studied. As the Temple began to play a greater role in the religious identity, there came a need to codify more rules of conduct and rules to maintain ritual purity. But throughout this process, the Decalogue retained an important role. It reminded each generation to focus on the two relationships that mattered, with God and with neighbor. Christians, usually after much personal struggle, realize that the answer to the meaning of life is not found in a tidy set of words, but rather in a relationship with God. And like human relationships, the one with God can be more opaque than clear; the relationship with God must include a relationship with all creation, including women and men. The reality is that relationships can be messy.

Christians believe that the hopes and promises of the Old Testament were fulfilled in Jesus' life, death, and resurrection. His preaching of God's coming kingdom offered people the choice to let God truly become the center and focus of their existence. In that offer, they found a faith that permitted them to live with forgiveness from sin, courage to break stereotypes, and freedom from demons, illness, discrimination, and so forth. Christians are aware that Jesus lived in a culture that had its own religious history that shaped him; they draw inspiration and guidance from this history, which includes the Decalogue.

Today, Christians have the advantage of a long history of reflection, both theological and spiritual, on the Scripture and its connection with their lives. The chapters that comprise this book were written by experts in Scripture or moral theology and appeared as articles in *Liguorian* magazine in 2007 and 2008. Readers' positive reactions and requests to reprint the articles led Liguori to compile them in this book. All of these authors write with an eye to educating the reader, helping us to see the relevance of the Ten Commandments and the Church's tradition of reflecting on the inspired Word of God. An introduction, conclusion, and "Bringing Home the Message" section with questions for reflection not written by the author of the original article will help deepen your understanding and appreciation of these insightful pieces.

The Redemptorists and staff at Liguori Publications are pleased to publish this work. We hope the contents offer insights and direction about how contemporary Christians can live the Ten Commandments with an integrity that honors the commitment made by our ancestors in the faith. In a society that has GPS technology built into cell phones and cars, we always know where we are and how long it will take to reach our destination. For those who are spiritually lost, and even for those who believe they are following God's will, the Ten Commandments are a "Spiritual Positioning System" that tells us who we are and points us in the direction of who we might become.

1

I am the Lord your God; you shall have no other gods before me.

(CCC* 2084-2141)

*Catechism of the Catholic Church

Swept Up by Love: Living the First Commandment

Kevin J. O'Neil, C.Ss.R.

We all know how helpful boundaries can be. Drivers who find themselves becoming a bit drowsy on the road are grateful when they are roused from sleepiness by the sound of their tires on the ridged pavement along the edge of the highway. It alerts them that they have gone over the line and must get back into their lane. Similarly, a ship's captain must stay within the bounds of the channel lest the boat run aground. Sports fields are marked by areas that are inbounds and out-of-bounds, and players must abide by them. These markers are precisely that: markers delineating boundaries. They do not necessarily tell drivers how to excel at driving or captains how best to navigate the waters or athletes how to perform to perfection. They simply designate boundaries.

The "ten words" of Scripture, or the Ten Commandments as they have been called, serve a similar purpose. They voice the expectations or, to use a stronger word, the demands of a relationship. They clearly state what is out-of-bounds in our relationships with God and neighbor. But like the boundaries listed above, they do not necessarily tell us how to excel or be virtuous in these relationships.

While the Commandments often serve as a guide for an individual's examination of conscience prior to celebrating the sacrament of reconciliation and might be associated with a person's individual relationships with God and neighbor, it is helpful to keep in mind that the ten words were originally given to a community, to the people of Israel, by the God who had brought them out of Egypt. As we reflect on this commandment, then, we might think of its implications for us as individual believers and as members of a community.

In this brief chapter on the first word, I will begin by addressing what is out-of-bounds; then I will explore what it might mean to excel in fulfilling this commandment.

The most obvious prohibition of this command for the Israelite people, as well as for believers today, was against placing another god before the one true God. Scripture tells us that at the same time Moses was receiving the Ten Commandments from the Lord, the Israelites were fashioning a golden calf to worship—a clear violation of their relationship with the God who had freed them from slavery. (See Exodus 32:1–6.)

If the fear in Old Testament times was that the people of Israel would put their trust in gods other than the one true God, today we might rightly fear that "things" could become the objects of our trust, our hope, even our love. The danger of putting material goods, our professional life, our social standing and image, our national standing or geopolitical goals, or countless other things before God is a daily challenge for individuals and societies. This commandment calls us to what is primary as people created by and called to a relationship with God. The *Catechism of the Catholic Church* lists other things this commandment prohibits: superstition, idolatry, divination and magic, irreligion, atheism, and agnosticism. (See 2110–2128.) In one way or another, all of these place God in a secondary position, causing us to fail to recognize who God is in our lives.

In addition to the prohibitions mentioned in the Catechism, living out-of-bounds in our relationship with God touches other aspects of our personal and communal lives. We can claim to believe in God yet cling to an image of God that is not true to who God is. The French philosopher Voltaire commented that God created us in God's own image and that we have returned the compliment. Do we portray God as we want God to be or in the way that God really is to the best of our knowledge and belief?

What false gods—or more precisely, what incomplete images of God—must we abandon to love the God who truly is? God the Lawgiver? God the Judge? Although these titles capture some truth of who God is, they will ultimately lead to a poor relationship with God if they become our principal image of God. Certainly, God's will is that we should follow the Commandments, but God is more than one who says "do this...don't do that." God is rightly called judge in that the difference between right and wrong and the truth that lies in our hearts are clearer to no one more than God, yet God's primary stance toward us is not one of judge. Other incomplete and false images of God are also out-of-bounds. I'd like to focus on one false image that is particularly important for us today as a community, as a nation.

In the Old Testament, God is frequently portrayed as a warrior, as one who is out to destroy the enemy. Has this false image of God been debunked, or do we still believe that God delights in the suffering and death of the "enemy," however we might define that term? As a nation, do we believe that God delights in the death of those who oppose us or that God sides with us and against those whom we oppose in violent wars? Does God's option for the poor imply a disdain for the wealthy? Does God's love of all life imply that God hates those who opt for an abortion or champion the death penalty? Do we really believe that these sentiments lie in the heart of God?

Any image of God that allows for hatred or disdain or disrespect or vengeance to dwell in God's heart is false and is out-of-bounds according to the first commandment. Similarly, any image of God that would allow these sentiments to dwell in the hearts of those made in God's image and likeness is false. A true image of God is one that recognizes that God's stance can be nothing but love toward all persons, even in the face of the worst brutalities we humans inflict on one another. God wants only our good—ours and everyone else's on this planet. God's stance of love toward all people does not change.

To have "no other gods before me" means, then, not simply to avoid atheism, irreligion, materialism, and the like. It also means to dispel incomplete and false images of God that present obstacles to worshiping the true God and living fully the life to which we are called by the first commandment. We must believe in and worship God as God truly is.

One of the lines of sacred Scripture with the most far-reaching implications is "God is love" (1 John 4:16). This brief description of God, the theme of Pope Benedict XVI's first encyclical, captures wonderfully the God whom we are invited to love. God loves us not because of who we are or because of anything we have done; God loves us because of who God is. Love like this makes no sense to us, whose love for others often comes with countless conditions. Saint Alphonsus, along with Saint Catherine of Siena and others, called God's love for us "crazy," unreasonable, even inexplicable. Yet God loves us.

To excel in living out the first commandment is to allow ourselves to be swept up by God's love and to love God in return. Spending quiet time in prayer, worshiping God in community at Sunday Mass, and reading the Bible to learn of the countless ways God has reached out to us are all ways that we may come to know God, who loves us completely.

The Catechism speaks of nurturing the virtues of faith, hope, and charity in our relationship with God. (See 2087–2094.) Faith is our response to this God who loves us and ultimately holds us in his care. Hope moves us to trust in God's love for us, acknowledging who we are before God and living with confidence in God's presence and action in our lives. And finally, charity is allowing the love of God to abide in us, responding to God's love and being instruments of that love.

"The first commandment enjoins us to love God above everything and [to love] all creatures for him and because of him" (*CCC* 2093). This unbreakable connection between loving God and loving God's creatures, especially one another, is found in the same text of Scripture as "God is love": "Those who say, 'I love God,' and hate their brothers or sisters, are liars; for those who do not love a brother or sister whom they have seen, cannot love God whom they have not seen. The commandment we have from him is this: those who love God must love their brothers and sisters also" (1 John 4:20–21). Saint Thomas Aquinas expressed the same sentiment in a different way. He said that to love someone is to make that person's loves our own. To love God is to make God's loves our own.

To know God and to love God bring the further demand of loving one another. As people made in God's image and likeness, we must "get God right" in the sense of worshiping a true God, then relate to one another as God relates to us. God loves nothing more than us, his daughters and sons. As individuals and as a community, we fulfill this commandment not merely when we love God but when our love for God moves us to a deep love, compassion, and just action for God's people.

So we might ask ourselves where our worship of God leads us. Does it move us to a deeper appreciation of God's unconditional love? Does it move us to make God's loves our own? Does it move us from our quiet time and our community time with God to a concern, love, and action for God's people, our neighbors near and far?

To be swept up by God's love is to live with faith, hope, and love for this "crazy" God who loves us and to be similarly crazy, even unreasonable, in the way that we love one another. To love God with our whole heart and soul and mind and strength is most clearly demonstrated through our worship of God and our action on behalf of God's loves. Fulfilling the first commandment surely entails staying inbounds, but the fullness of life to which we are called invites us to receive God's unconditional love, to return it to God, and to allow it to flow into the world through us.

■ ■ ■

Bringing Home the Message

For any of the commandments to make a difference, we must engage in self-reflection. This means we need to examine our lives and be honest about what we do with our time, money, and even what we do with the emotional, physical, and mental components of life. It means asking hard questions in search of answers that we might not like to hear because they will tell us that we're neither as generous nor as tolerant as we think we are. In these times of candor lies the path to growth.

True, the first commandment challenges us to look at such false gods as material goods, status, and so forth, but the author injects a deeper concern when he writes, "We can claim to believe in God yet cling to an image of God that is not true to who God is." This is also true when we look at our own parents! How might you have felt when you discovered that your dad couldn't put a spin on a football, or your mom was not able to give you the same dosage of kindness that your friends' mothers doled out? The fact of our parents' limitations forces us to recast what being a good parent might mean.

As we become mature Christians, we must reconsider our image of God and how expansive it is. Keeping the first commandment means we will edit our definitions of God, as our capacity to love enlarges. Christian love is not a love that allows libertine behavior with no boundaries, because Christian love speaks in the language of sacrifice. We give up those values that devalue what's good and true; we give up images of God that reinforce gender or racial barriers and prevent the progress of peoples and countries. As we leave this brief study of the first commandment, we see that it is more than prohibition against worshipping other gods. At the heart, it's a call to understand and practice a kind of love that engages in the discipline to keep alive a nourishing relationship with God who is with us not just on Sundays, but every day.

What are you willing to live for, and what are you willing to die for? Can you find God in the answers to these questions? Who are the other gods that make a claim on your time and money? How do these other gods interfere with your ability to build a life that is consistent with your beliefs? What might you change to be back "in bounds"?

2

You shall not take the name of the Lord your God in vain.

(CCC 2142-2167)

Living Up to the Name of God: The Second Commandment

Stephen T. Rehrauer, C.Ss.R.

The second of the Ten Commandments forbids taking God's name in vain. It describes both a negative behavior to be avoided and a value to be revered and realized. In the two places in which it appears in the Hebrew Scriptures (Exodus 20:7; Deuteronomy 5:11), the second commandment is a logical extension of the first, which recognizes the truth that there is one—and only one—God, revealed to the people of Israel. In the teachings of Jesus Christ, the positive aspect of the second commandment appears when Jesus teaches us to pray that God's name be hallowed. (See Matthew 6:9–14.)

Names in Scripture communicate an essential characteristic of a person. The names of people change as a result of their encounter with the Divine, demonstrating that once we encounter God, we are no longer the same person. Abram becomes Abraham, Sarai becomes Sarah, Jacob becomes Israel, Simon becomes Peter, Saul becomes Paul. With the new name come both an identity and a responsibility. The new man or woman, changed as a result of coming to know God, is expected to live up to the name's meaning.

By revealing the divine name of YHWH to them, God entered into a personal relationship with the people of Israel, which made them a holy people. Unlike the surrounding nations, who lived in the ignorance of worshiping many gods of their own making and naming, the people of Israel were gifted with not only knowledge of the true God but also an intimacy with this God. Knowing God's name, they could call upon God for help. And God was adamant that their identity as a people was part of God's name. " 'The Lord, the God of your ancestors, the God of Abraham, the God of Isaac, and the God of Jacob, has sent me to you': This is my name forever, and this my title for all generations" (Exodus 3:15). The people of Israel were God's possession, and their name was now a part of God's eternal and unchanging name.

The gift of knowing the divine name was an eloquent expression of God's promise and plan for salvation at work in human history, and of humanity's part in this plan. Knowing God's name changed the very identity of the people who now possessed that name. God not only revealed to them the divine name of YHWH but bestowed that name upon them as a "people," joining them together as a nation by the knowledge of this name and what it signified: they were "Yahweh's people," and the purpose of their existence was to reveal Yahweh to the nations so that God's name would be known and revered. This had clear consequences for the way in which each individual member of the Hebrew community was to give form and shape to his or her life. The same is true for those of us who have been baptized in Christ and given the name Christian. As 1 John 3:1–3 reminds us, we are in fact children of God, and taking the name "God's children" has serious implications for how we are to live, both individually and socially.

The ancient Hebrews took this commandment so seriously that they were forbidden from even speaking God's name except under strict religious ritual conditions. This practice respected the letter of the divine Law. Yet the Law's deeper spirit is developed throughout the entire Hebrew Scriptures and comes to fruition powerfully in the teachings of Jesus as he fulfills and completes both the Law and the Prophets. The Book of Exodus reminds us that God is powerfully transcendent and holy, far beyond anything we could ever imagine or understand. As bearers of the divine name, God's people are also to be holy, set apart to glorify God by the way they live. The Book of Deuteronomy, written at a time when God's people were returning from exile, reminds the people of their purpose as a nation. They are to be unique among all the peoples on earth so that others will come to know the true God through their example.

Both of these written presentations of the second commandment were highly influenced by the preaching of the prophets, whose central emphasis was on loving fidelity to God and to the meaning of what it is to be God's people in concrete action. God is revealed in word and deed. Respect for God's name among the people who bear that name and who are charged with revealing that name to the nations prohibits specific behaviors and requires others.

At its face value, the second commandment forbids us to ask God for frivolous favors or to place responsibility for what we ourselves do on God's shoulders or to use God as an excuse or a remedy for the results of our failures or foolish or selfish actions. Thinking that the name of God exists to serve us rather than recognizing that we exist to bear witness to the name of God is the essence of vanity. The use of God's name must be reserved for things that are truly important.

Prophets and all others who speak in God's name are charged to speak truly. (See Deuteronomy 18:15–22.) To presume to speak in God's name without having been given the authority to do so, or having been given the authority, to speak in God's name without a true intimacy that leads to an authentic knowledge of God; to presume to put our own words into God's mouth or to use God's name to harm or destroy other human beings, whom God also loves; these are all common ways of violating the second commandment. Worse still is to use God's name to engender anger or hatred, to divide people rather than unite them in love, to motivate people to engage in destructive violence, or as a club with which to wound.

To call upon the name of God to support us in activities that are contrary to the very nature of God as Divine Goodness, as Father, as Source of Truth, as Love, as Creator, as Redeemer, is vanity. To ask God to support us in a lie as in the case of perjury, to ask God to strike down our enemies in cruelty, or to condemn someone to hell for all eternity when God wishes all people to be saved is to insult the goodness and mercy of God. Doing so not only asks God to do our will in contrast to God's will but it reveals that we do not truly know the God we are calling upon and are assuming an intimacy with God that we obviously do not truly possess.

Jesus places this aspect of the commandment in harsh relief when he forbids us to take oaths of any kind, suggesting that instead of swearing by heaven or earth, we simply tell the truth. (See Matthew 5:33–37.) He reminds us that not everyone who prophesies or does mighty deeds in his name or cries out "Lord" will enter the kingdom of heaven. (See Matthew 7:21–23.) He has harsh words of condemnation for the Pharisees, who teach as divine laws the mere human conventions they themselves created. (See Matthew 5:20.) He is clear that his true mother and brothers and sisters are those who live the will of our heavenly Father. (See Matthew 12:46–50.)

The second commandment also has social implications for what must be done. In its deeper and more positive sense it was a call to the Israelite community to live their identity as the people who bore God's name. The resident alien living among them was to be welcomed and treated well. They were to be honest in their business dealings with one another. They were to tithe so that no one among them lived in need. They were to care for the widow, the orphan, and the dispossessed. They were to live justly. These were the ways they would honor the name of Yahweh. (See Jeremiah 7:1–11.) This is what it meant to be Yahweh's people.

Permitting poverty, hunger, oppression, and injustice to remain in their midst would have reflected badly upon God, whose name they bore. And speaking through the prophets, God was adamant that those who ignored these obligations or perverted them would call upon God's name and not be heard. (See Isaiah 58.) The second commandment had to be written upon their hearts and lived in their deeds. The tablet of stone had to be replaced with a heart of flesh. If not, their name would be changed from Yahweh's people to "not my people" (Hosea 1:8).

Jesus taught that all of the Law could be summarized in two main commands: to love God and to love our neighbor. In the Gospel of John, Jesus reminds us that it is precisely by the way in which we love one another that we are known as his disciples. (See 3:31–35.) A major violation of the spirit of the second commandment occurs each and every time we who bear the name Christian fail to love one another. The second commandment forms for us a bridge between knowledge of the one true God definitively revealed in Jesus Christ and our life as members of a community joined and formed into oneness by that knowledge. The first commandment is to love God. The second commandment is to love our neighbor, because we cannot love God and hate our neighbor at the same time. (See 1 John 4:7–21.) To do so is to take the Lord's name—which defines who we are and how we are to live—in vain.

The spirit of the second commandment comes to its clearest and deepest expression, however, in the Our Father. (See Matthew 6:9–14.) In the first line of this prayer, Jesus teaches us to address God as "our Father," a term of love and intimacy. The second line of the prayer expresses the second commandment: may God's name be kept holy. The third line tells us how: in living as members of God's kingdom by doing the Father's will on earth.

For the followers of Jesus Christ, who by baptism become members of God's people and children of the heavenly Father, the second commandment is a call to live our Christian dignity in this world by intentionally focusing our lives and activities around God's will. It is a positive call and a prayer to be worthy of the name Christian, with which we have been gifted. And this of course requires that we cultivate a personal intimacy with God our Father so that we can indeed come to know and understand God's will.

Christians truly live the teaching of the gospel when we care for the sick, clothe the naked, visit those in prison, feed the hungry, forgive one another in our hearts, love our enemies, and do good to those who persecute us. When we hunger and thirst for justice, show mercy, act as peacemakers, proclaim the good news of Christ's salvation in word and deed, then our heavenly Father is glorified and his name is held holy on earth. To do any less or any differently and call ourselves followers of Christ and children of the Father is vanity.

■ ■ ■

Bringing Home the Message

Living the second commandment requires more than not swearing. As is true of the other commandments, it moves us in a direction of life. Because God has initiated a relationship with us, we are now members of a community, a faith community that works to achieve its purpose as it practices what it preaches. More than one contemporary Christian has remarked on the Church's inability to influence contemporary society and shape an understanding of humanity that promotes its dignity. There is more work to do.

Every age needs to embrace God's gift of self and respond to that invitation, thus it is a fact that the community is always in a process of rebirth. We need to teach young people that God is holy and so are we; we need to align our acts with our faith and become witnesses to a love that can abolish verbal (and physical) abuse of others. The second commandment is not archaic; rather it is a testament to the power of words and the relationship that can be deepened through a thoughtful stance in all we say and do.

There is a saying in Spanish: *Del dicho al hecho hay un gran trecho.* ("Easier said than done.") Much of our daily activity is built on trusting another person's words. A neighbor agrees to pick up the children at school. A business leader agrees—first in words, then in writing—to provide a product or service. To engage in earnest conversation is to reveal part of ourselves to another person; it extends to the other person an invitation of trust that what is shared will be honored and the information will be used in a manner that respects our dignity. Our daily work has a holy dimension to it. The author of this chapter writes, "The spirit of the second commandment comes to its clearest and deepest expression, however, in the Our Father." Why would he say this?

To go deeper, ask yourself: Are there any words or names that evoke a sense of awe in me? What are they? Who do I know who reflects a strong, holy presence? What makes that person "holy"? Is it what they say or what they do? What will I do to better live out the second commandment?

3

Remember the sabbath day, to keep it holy.

(*CCC* 2168-2195)

Rest, Worship, and Community: Living the Third Commandment

Timothy E. O'Connell, PhD

Rebecca had the right idea. She and Saul, observant Jews, took the Sabbath very seriously.

"I feel sad for those who don't have the Sabbath practice," she said to me. "I know some people think our Sabbath practice is a rule that burdens us. But I think it's a wonderful gift! I don't think I could survive without this weekly time to get off the treadmill. Sabbath is when we talk, when we plan, when we think, when we remind ourselves of what life is all about. How do you folks get along without that sacred time?"

"Remember the sabbath day, and keep it holy" (Exodus 20:8). The third commandment, like all the commandments, is not some fee exacted by God as the price of his care for us. Rather, it is gift. Woven together, the Ten Commandments are a great, inspired poem, drawing lines around a way of living that can make us whole and keep us holy, a way of living that in the end is the only way we can be happy.

The genius of the Ten Commandments—what makes them such a wonderful gift of God—is not that any one of the items is so surprising. Rather, the genius is the tight, clear way they sketch hard-won wisdom of life. We are not forced to spend a lifetime finding this wisdom; it is given to us on a platter. Live like this, the commandments say, and you will truly, fully live.

In the tapestry of the Ten Commandments, the third has a special place, sitting on the cusp between the first series with its direct focus on our relationship to God and the second series with its focus on our relationships to one another. The third commandment looks in both directions. It starts with rest. Then it calls us to worship. Finally, it points us to community. Let's look at each of these elements.

REST

As we move through the many books of the Bible, the opening texts of Genesis are never far from our attention. This third commandment is a great example. The epic creation story of Genesis tells us of how we come from God. Six days it took God to shape creation. All of it—all that we are and all that we experience—comes from the hand of love itself. All is drawn out of nothingness, lifted into the light, brought to life, and pointed to fulfillment. The great work of creation, we call it. How complex! How wondrous! How truly cosmic!

How exhausting? Of course, God never really gets tired. But somehow, as the inspired storytellers of Genesis imagined the work of creation, they could not imagine it without a pause of rest. And so they tell us, "...he rested on the seventh day" (Genesis 2:2).

Why rest? There is an astonishing rhythm to how things work in the created world. I don't pretend to understand it, but I know it is true. This rhythm involves two moments: effort and rest.

These two opposing actions strengthen muscles. In the world of physical fitness, the experts give this advice: exercise to fatigue and then take a day to recuperate. Skip either part of this rhythm and the goal will not be achieved.

Similarly, in the aesthetic world, scholars tell us that the beauty of music is built through the alternation of stress and release, dissonance and harmony. If everything is gentle, the music quickly becomes boring. But if the tension is never released, it becomes excruciating in the end. And the beauty of all the other art forms comes about similarly, through the alternation of tension and release.

The rightness of this rhythm is visible throughout the fabric of life. The Gospel of Luke tells the wonderful story of Jesus' visit to Mary and Martha. (See 10:38–42.) Martha is busy with the preparations and complains to Jesus that Mary isn't helping. Jesus replies, of course, "Mary has chosen the better part, which will not be taken from her."

Overly simple explanations of this story suggest that Mary was in the right and Martha in the wrong, but we know otherwise. Without Martha, everyone would starve. And Jesus does not say that Martha is wrong. He simply says that her effort is not the most important thing. The most important thing is being together. The activity is in service to the relationship, not the other way around. And that is something one must never forget.

Like all biblical stories, this tale is really about us. We are Mary and Martha. We are work and rest. We are achievement and contemplation. Both are needed. Both are good. And, alas, both can be temptations. Mary's simplicity can turn into presumption. Her wonder in the presence of the divine can slide into boredom. At the same time, Martha's anxious activity can turn to arrogance, a sense of preeminent importance. It can also turn into its dark opposite: depression at overwhelming and endless tasks.

So the lesson becomes clear. For six days do your best. And on the seventh day rest, trust, enjoy. Let the rhythm of your life remind you that, in the end, your value does not come from your productivity. It comes from the very fact that you are a creature of a loving God, good and beautiful in yourself.

What is the look of this rest? It will vary for each one of us. But whatever it is, if it is Sabbath rest, it will look surprisingly like worship.

HOLY WORSHIP

That wonderful story of Mary and Martha makes clear that rest is not for its own sake. Mary's part is better not because it is easier; rather, it is better because it provides the chance to be with Jesus. This rest, this leisure, is a tool to be used to attune us to the truths of reality. And paramount among those truths is this: God is God—and we are not! So rest is really a way of describing worship.

I once knew a very wise and holy priest who refused to assign prayers as a "penance" for Catholics going to confession. His reason? He said this: "I don't assign pleasant things as penance. I don't assign having a fancy dinner or going to a concert or taking a nap, so why should I assign that pleasant thing called communing with God? Praying is not a penance; it's a treat!"

At its deepest level, worship is simply the act of basking in the beauty of truth. An astute spiritual guide advised her followers to take on a simple pious practice. "When you get up," she said, "open the window shade, face the east where the sun is coming up, and bow deeply. Hold that posture for a moment. Then go about your day!"

It is no surprise, then, that the third commandment does not merely say, "Remember the Sabbath day." Rather, it says, "Remember the sabbath day, to keep it holy." Let the delight of your rest include the delight of worship.

That worship, like all restful activities, will take different forms for each of us. For many people it involves getting outside, escaping the pressure of office and the chores of home, and communing with nature. It may involve a gentle walk or an energetic run. It may find us riding a bike or paddling a canoe, quietly weeding a garden or playing an intense set of tennis.

For other people worship involves something more aesthetic. Perhaps it will be as an audience member listening to a symphony, walking through an art gallery, or taking an architectural tour around the city. Or it may be the more active role of a participant, playing one's piano or guitar, sketching or knitting, diving deep into the mysteries of Sudoku, singing or dancing, or struggling to speak one's soul beautifully through lines of poetry.

No matter how one does it, such rest-worship inevitably speaks two truths. On the one hand, it makes manifest the truth of our intrinsic goodness: even when we are not productive or useful, we have goodness and worth. On the other hand, it affirms the truth of God's love, even when we do not expect it, even when we may not deserve it.

That rest-worship contemplates God's love, tastes it, and enjoys it. And in so doing, it confirms it. And so, in this worship, whether the words are actually spoken or not, our hearts speak the ultimate prayer: "Thank you, God!"

COMMUNITY CARE

It may surprise you that no mention has yet been made of the obligation to attend Mass. Isn't that at the heart of the third commandment? No. The issue of common worship must come at the end of our discussion, not at the beginning.

"Why do I have to go to Mass?" asked the teenager. "I feel much closer to God standing at the edge of a lake or reading a poem."

The teenager is, of course, telling the truth. It is a rare liturgy, indeed, that can compete with the beauty of creation in evoking the wonder of God. In fact, as much as I love the liturgies in my parish, they can't compete with the view of the Grand Canyon, of waves on Lake Michigan, or of thunderclouds racing across the sky. In fact, some weeks, when the singing is weak, when the preaching is uninspired, when babies cry, and when the sound system fails, these liturgies can't compete with a walk down the street.

So the command to keep holy the Sabbath does not immediately lead to an expectation of shared liturgy. We Catholics have to be clear on this. It first leads only to rest and to worship of the heart. To understand the expectation of common worship, another insight must be added.

The teenager asked, "Why must I go to Mass when I feel closer to God out in nature?" And the wise adult answered, "Because if you worship God out in nature all by yourself, it does me no good!"

The truth is that sometimes life is gentle enough that the beauty of nature and genius of art are sufficient to remind us of God. But not always. Sometimes life brings pain or suffering, failure or vileness. And when this happens, God can seem very far away, indeed. How do we cope with those dark nights? Well, with help from our friends, we get by at such times. What keeps me strong and gives me hope in troubled times is knowing that others experience God and find strength and consolation in the presence of the divine—what keeps me going is you!

We feed on one another's faith, sometimes offering the nourishment and sometimes being nourished. And together, as a band of pilgrims, we find our way through life. Psychologists point out that the human person is essentially social. What that means is really very simple: we cannot be alone! Even when I am by myself, within seconds I think of the other people in my life. I think of them, I imagine them, and in the magical power of imagination they join me wherever I am. In imagination, where we most fully live, it is never me; it is always we.

From the moment of birth until the instant of death, we are woven into a fabric of community. We need one another. For food and shelter, for productivity and meaning, we need one another, giving and receiving, helping and being helped, in an endless circle of sharing.

Imagine that you come to a moment in life where all hope seems lost, all possibilities have been spent. But with a single last effort of hope, you drag yourself to church. Alas, this is the week all the rest of us have decided to take time off! You enter the front door, but no one is there. You wait for the ceremony to begin, but only a deadly silence presents itself. You would give up, I wager. You would walk out the door and never come back. For at the single moment when you needed us, we were not there for you.

Thank God that this is not how it happens. Instead, at that moment of need you enter the church and you find kindred spirits. Not saints, to be sure, but other pilgrims, also struggling to find their way. Indeed, at this moment, they may be having success in their lives. They may not really need to be at Mass, but they are there, nonetheless. Just in case this may be your moment of need, they are there. For you, they are there.

I hope that on some other Sunday, when their moment of need arrives, it will be you who are there for them. When that happens, we will finally have learned in the full how to keep holy the Sabbath.

■ ■ ■

Bringing Home the Message

Have you noticed how the day's activities and energy have now crept into the nighttime? With electricity and lights we can pore over work at home on computers. Rest is a scarce commodity, and it's difficult to become mentally and physically quiet. What do we do? Ask the doctor for a prescription drug to help us sleep? And if this isn't enough, technology puts us in constant contact with friends and colleagues. The author of this chapter makes a strong point about the rhythm of effort and rest found in God's creative movement. One measure of maturity is the self-awareness required to observe when we are not living healthily and the discipline to make changes to destructive behaviors.

Where the third commandment leads us today is back to ourselves, asking us to question how authentically we embrace the relationship God initiated with us. We are co-creators with God, and a healthy balance between shouldering the effort of work and accepting the restorative support found in beauty, community, and worship is essential. For after all, life is a marathon, not a sprint.

Think through your days and weeks, and look for a pattern to your effort-rest rhythm. Do you have a default mode? For example, when you have free time after the laundry is done, the bills are paid, and dinner is made and served, what's the first thing you do? Check for new email or text messages? Even when these things aren't completed, can you take time to recharge? How does participating in Mass influence your effort-rest rhythm? Do you find it difficult to be quiet and be present to God in silence? Are you ready to "Go in peace to love and serve the Lord," or are you content to say you've fulfilled your obligation?

This chapter's author writes, "The teenager asked, 'Why must I go to Mass when I feel closer to God out in nature?' And the wise adult answered, 'Because if you worship God out in nature all by yourself, it does me no good!'" How would you respond to the teenager? What kind of answer might you give that would invite him or her to feel the strength of the worshipping community?

4

**Honor
your father and
your mother.**

(CCC 2197-2257)

Fathers and Mothers, Sons and Daughters: Living the Fourth Commandment

Mara Kelly-Zukowski, PhD

The Ten Commandments, or what is often referred to as the Decalogue, is actually composed of two sets. The first two commandments make up the first set and focus on our relationship with God—our "vertical" duties. The second set (which includes commandments four through ten) focuses on our relationships with one another—our "horizontal" duties. The third commandment, as Timothy E. O'Connell explains in chapter three of this book, sits on the cusp between the two sets. It looks in both directions: toward God and toward other people.

The fourth commandment sets the tone in the second set of commandments in a number of different ways. First of all, it describes the most basic of all human relationships: that between a child and parent. Second, it provides a firm basis on which subsequent proscribed behavior is designed to rest. In other words, those who honor their fathers and mothers will usually not be prone to breaking any of the other commandments.

In the ancient Israelite culture, the law of honoring one's father and mother was key to the establishment of a long-lasting and stable civilization. Given to the wandering Israelites in the midst of their long and loosely structured desert experience, the commandments were a way of solidifying them into a society that would ultimately settle down and thrive in the land promised to their forefather Abraham. By asserting that the "rules" of individual families rested on the honor of the parents by the children, God was ensuring that the family would become the microcosm of a greater society and a mirror of the relationship that God, as parent, was establishing with God's adopted sons and daughters. "In creating man and woman, God instituted the human family and endowed it with its fundamental constitution.....For the common good of its members and of society, the family necessarily has manifold responsibilities, rights, and duties" (*Catechism of the Catholic Church*, 2203).

In Hebrew, a special word was used for this "honor": *kavod*. It is interesting that the word love doesn't appear in the Decalogue, just the term *kavod*. It is a positive term; indeed, this commandment is the only one in the second table that is worded positively as a duty to be obeyed rather than a behavior to be shunned. It involved respecting one's parents, which the Hebrew Bible defines as obeying them, refraining from insulting or striking them, behaving in a disrespectful manner toward them, and misappropriating their property. (See Exodus 21:15, 17; Leviticus 20:9; Deuteronomy 27:16; Proverbs 30:17.)

However, it also included caring for them in their old age. (See Proverbs 23:22.) *Kavod* outlined a relationship that was to extend from birth to death—one that sometimes involved a change in concrete obligations to one's parents but one that never allowed the child to neglect the parents' particular needs. In fact, Jesus harshly rebuked his fellow countrymen who neglected their duty to care for their parents, even if it was done in the name of religious duties. (See Matthew 15:3–6.)

Following the commandment to honor our parents is especially difficult when our relationship with our parents changes, as is bound to happen during the natural process of growing up. As young children, we honor our parents by obeying their instructions, talking to them respectfully, and recognizing (to whatever extent we're able) that what they do for us and ask of us is for our own good.

As adolescents, honoring our parents involves appreciating that their rules (even those we rebel against) are motivated by their love for us. These rules were constructed to protect us and give us the boundaries that would allow us to flourish. Rather than focusing on the rules themselves, this commandment asks us to focus on the deep-seated love that rule-giving parents obviously have for us.

As adults, the ground again shifts under our feet. Since we often possess more physical strength (and perhaps more mental agility) than our parents, we have a tendency to want to reverse our roles and become parents to our aging mothers and fathers. When we do this, we treat our parents as unruly children who do not fulfill their obligations to obey our commands. We become impatient, patting ourselves on the back for attending to what we perceive to be their needs (which really may not be), and feeling resentful that they don't seem to appreciate our noble gestures.

Such an attitude certainly does not reflect the honor due them. At this stage in our lives, honoring our parents might involve the simple commitment of time: spending an afternoon with them, inviting them to dinner as one would a friend, or phoning frequently to share each other's lives more intimately. In a day and age when the population is living much longer than our ancestors, the later years are often lonely ones. What better respect and honor can we give our parents who sacrificed much of their lives for us than making their long days a little less lonely?

The honor with which we, as children, should treat our parents reflects their dignity, the fact that they were created and are loved by God. When we recognize one another's dignity, it guards against a feeling of superiority when we deign to provide an act of kindness. This dignity is not only present when our parents are in their prime but also when they become elderly, slow, unsteady on their feet, short in patience, or perhaps even incontinent. Dignity does not depend on bodily strength or the ability to control one's bodily functions. It is inherent within each of us and must be treated with honor. "My child, help your father in his old age, and do not grieve him as long as he lives; even if his mind fails, be patient with him; because you have all your faculties do not despise him" (Sirach 3:12). By doing this, children "contribute to the growth in holiness of their parents. Each and everyone should be generous and tireless in forgiving one another for offenses, quarrels, injustices, and neglect. Mutual affection suggests this. The charity of Christ demands it" (*CCC* 2227).

Of course, the *kavod*, or honor, required by the fourth commandment must ultimately be based on love, for as the great Jewish philosopher Maimonides observed, it is through love that one can view another as deserving of honor and respect. "The respect of children, whether minors or adults, for their father and mother is nourished by the natural affection born of the bond uniting them" (*CCC* 2214).

The great poet Maya Angelou once asked, "How do you react when your child enters the room? Do your eyes light up?" In the same way that we parents watched our children sleeping, staring at them with a mixture of awe, wonder, and delight, so too should we continue to be filled with wonder and delight at the sight of those we love as they move to new stages in their lives. We need to relish our children's individuality, the persons into whom they're maturing each day. We need to recapture that feeling of awe at the mere sight of them and manifest that feeling so overtly that they immediately know how loved they are. We should regard our parents in the same way, not focusing on their increasing biological weaknesses, but standing in awe as we remember the incredible love they have shown us day after day, month after month, and year after year. Doing this will make it all the easier to honor them in the biblical sense of the term.

This does not mean, however, that one always feels affection for the object of honor. The love on which *kavod* is based does not necessarily involve an emotional feeling. It can best be described as the love (or, in Greek, *agape*) of which Jesus often spoke in the Second Testament. It is a love that is volitional, based on a decision to love rather than on a feeling of love. It is a love that makes its possessor determined to take care of a person's real needs, regardless of what he or she feels about that person at the moment. It is a selfless love that resolves to look after another before considering our own needs or desires. It is the highest love to which we are called, the love about which Jesus said, "Just as I have loved you, you also should love one another" (John 13:34). It is also the love Jesus manifested when, suspended in agony from the cross, his primary concern was that his mother be cared for. With one of his last breaths he entrusted her care to his beloved disciple John. (See John 19:26–27.)

This agapeic love must start with the attitude of the parents toward their children. "Parents must regard their children as children of God and respect them as human persons" (*CCC* 2222). This by no means implies that there can be no correction and no discipline. An integral part of the agapeic love that Jesus practiced is ascertaining what is best for the other person. It is not in the best interest of a child to indulge him or her and to withhold the discipline that is needed to foster the child's self-discipline. Teaching a child that there are limits and consequences to transgressing those limits is usually much more difficult for the parent, but ultimately more beneficial to the child. "The Lord disciplines those whom he loves" (Hebrews 12:5–6). But we must also recall another admonition in Scripture: "Fathers, do not provoke your children, or they may lose heart" (Colossians 3:21).

The fourth commandment also has implications for the relationships we need to foster within our own communities—within the family of the Church and within the global community. It is specifically addressed to children referring to their relationships with their parents because, of all relationships, this is the prototype. It is a universally understood relationship that can be applied to those in the extended family, clan, race, and species. The fourth commandment asks us to regard all of our elders as "parents" and all of the younger members of society as our "children."

To do this will be the first step toward healing the wounds of division. For instance, it would be difficult to wage war on other people if we saw them as our parents and children. As the Catechism points out, this commandment "constitutes one of the foundations of the social doctrine of the Church." It applies to "elders and ancestors....It extends to the duties of pupils to teachers, employees to employers, subordinates to leaders, citizens to their country, and to those who administer or govern it," while presupposing the duties of those who exercise such authority to reciprocate in kind. (See *CCC* 2198–2199.) Seen in this way, the family is indeed the "original cell of social life" (*CCC* 2207).

The fourth commandment should also be a reflection of our own interaction with the Almighty. The family relationship is one of those vestiges of the Trinity of which Augustine spoke. "The Christian family is a communion of persons, a sign and image of the communion of the Father and the Son in the Holy Spirit. In the procreation and education of children it reflects the Father's work of creation" (*CCC* 2205). God, as loving parent who wants only the best for his or her children, must be accorded the honor, or *kavod*, that we should direct toward our earthly parents. We must honor God's role as parent, creator, and teacher and complete the cycle of honor that is the design of God from the beginning of time.

Finally, the fourth commandment is also the only commandment that has a reward attached for those who adhere to its precepts. It concludes with the words "that your days may be long in the land that the Lord your God is giving you." This does not mean that one who follows this law will live to a ripe old age. The focus is on "the land" and refers to the right of children to their fathers' land, but only if they have shown honor for their parents by caring and providing for them. It was an unfortunate part of that culture (and, some would argue, our own culture) that those who were unable to contribute to society, either because of age or illness, were often not financially supported. In this commandment, God echoes this ancient legal covenant meant to protect the weakest of society—the *anawim*, or "little ones"—but extends it to the entire community.

Although exegetes are not certain what this reward of your days being "long in the land" means for modern times, it could be argued that, in this age of divided families and children estranged from their parents, it might refer to the long-lasting relationship within families that is bound to endure for those who adhere to the fourth commandment. Parents will be bound to their children, and their children to them, their days being long in the land.

■ ■ ■

Bringing Home the Message

As lifespans of eighty and ninety years become commonplace, the need to heed the fourth commandment asserts itself. Roles are reversed, and our parents come to depend on us; however, we're called to honor them and not do or say things that would undermine their dignity. We read in this chapter how the Hebrew term *kavod* had implications that included not taking our parents' property, in addition to not hitting or insulting them. The author importantly removes an emotional element of this honor and grounds its practice "on a decision to love rather than on a feeling of love."

An application of this commandment today must take into account how our country accords rights to children, as well as the cultural value of equality. If we are all equal, how can a parent claim to direct, much less correct, a child? And why should a child honor a parent when the wider society has leveled the relationship between parent and child to the extent that the parent, as a source of authority and wisdom, is at times devalued? The fourth commandment might be seen as irrelevant and out of touch with our contemporary understanding of equality and individual rights. But it's not.

The fullest lives are those lived in relationship, and we are reminded of a primary relationship with this commandment—that of a parent and child. An interdependence of one on the other quietly shifts over time, and with reflection one learns that a deep joy comes in learning how to give and receive *kavod*. How can you show honor to a parent today? What examples from other people's lives can help you apply this commandment to your own life? What are the rewards for faithfully living this command? How does it help one become a good, more mature person?

The author writes, "The fourth commandment also has implications for the relationships we need to foster within our own communities—within the family of the Church and within the global community." Does it surprise you that the commandment can be expanded to touch on this reality as well? Why or why not?

5

You shall
not kill.

(CCC 2258-2330)

Respect for Life: Living the Fifth Commandment

Kevin O'Neil, C.Ss.R.

Have you ever found yourself engaged in an endless question-and-answer "battle" with a child who is persistent in getting an answer to the question, Why? "Why do I have to eat my spinach?" "Because it's good for you!" "Why?" "Because it has vitamins that keep you healthy." "Why?" And the dialogue goes on and on, perhaps ending with "Because I said so!" Although we may become exasperated with the child's endless questioning (or cleverness in frustrating his or her parent), we might ultimately appreciate that the child is trying to get to the bottom of things, to the most basic reason of all.

Among the commandments that touch on our relationship with our neighbor, and with God for that matter, none is more foundational than "You shall not kill" (Exodus 20:13). Why? Because the fifth commandment is about the gift of life—the most fundamental and sacred gift that we possess as human beings. It underscores the indispensability of human life in the face of all other values and goods that we pursue. We delight in family holidays, vacations with loved ones, music and reading, sports and exercise, prayer and meditation, and many other human pursuits. However, we can enjoy none of them unless we are alive. The fifth commandment reminds us that we do not have the right to deprive ourselves or others of this precious gift.

In terms of the commandments, before those about fidelity in marriage, truthfulness, and respecting the loved ones and material goods of others, we are given the command not to kill—or, rather, to protect the lives of one another.

Let's think for a moment about various scenarios in which killing occurs: murder, self-defense, abortion, war, euthanasia, and so forth. Not surprisingly, Catholic tradition has made a distinction between the just and unjust taking of human life. Why?

Because we have the right to care for our own lives and for the lives of the defenseless innocent, tradition has addressed circumstances in which taking life might be considered just. So even though we have a strong presumption against violence, the Church teaches that people may legitimately defend themselves from someone who would do them harm, even to the point of taking the aggressor's life if that were necessary to protect their own lives. This right to self-defense extends also to the State so that nations may defend themselves against an aggressor. Again, the presumption is against violence. Going to war must meet criteria of justice. Finally, tradition has argued that in extreme circumstances—that is, when society has no other way to protect itself against a criminal—capital punishment may be morally acceptable. Pope John Paul II shaped the current teaching of the Church in suggesting that such situations are nearly nonexistent. He said that for all practical purposes, the death penalty is never morally acceptable. (See The Gospel of Life [*Evangelium Vitae*], 27 and 56; see also *Catechism of the Catholic Church*, 2267.)

If the above examples address the just taking of human life, what constitutes the unjust killing of another? The Church teaches that the direct taking of innocent human life, as in abortion and euthanasia, is always wrong. It is a violation of justice and charity toward the innocent life and deprives victims of God's most fundamental gift. In addition to abortion and euthanasia, the *Catechism of the Catholic Church* and other teachings list genocide, murder, and suicide among those types of killing that run contrary to human good and are morally wrong.

Notice that the terms abortion, euthanasia, murder, and suicide name particular ways in which human lives are taken and express a negative ethical judgment on the act. However we do not know what was in the heart of the person who killed in concrete circumstances. Why mention this point?

Jesus was frequently concerned not simply with what a person did but also with what was in his or her heart. So when he referred to this commandment, he said: "You have heard that it was said to those of ancient times, 'You shall not murder'; and 'whoever murders shall be liable to judgment.' But I say to you that if you are angry with a brother or sister, you will be liable to judgment; and if you insult a brother or sister, you will be liable to the council; and if you say, 'You fool,' you will be liable to the hell of fire" (Matthew 5:21–22). Certainly Jesus is adding more to the list of don'ts related to this commandment, and we will return to these, but he is also focusing on what is in the heart of a person who acts in a harmful way toward a neighbor. Is there anger? Pride? Disdain? Vengeance? Arrogance?

Sometimes the hearts of those who take another's life are not full of hatred but are broken in other ways: by pain, hopelessness, loneliness, suffering, feelings of having no way out, and the like. Pope John Paul II recognized this fact in The Gospel of Life when he wrote that sometimes a woman who seeks an abortion is seeking important values like her own health or decent living conditions for her other family members. Sometimes she fears that the conditions the child would live in once born would be such that it would be better if the birth did not occur. (See *EV* 58.) Sometimes people who take their own lives or who help others to take their lives have good intentions.

In all of these instances, the person simply chooses a wrong way to achieve peace, for themselves or for others.

When dealing with the fifth commandment, the Church is clear that the taking of innocent life is always wrong; still, it recognizes that people do not always think, feel, or judge rightly and, consequently, make bad judgments for themselves and others, with disastrous consequences. Only God knows the full degree of their personal responsibility.

Jesus' words of caution about what lies in our hearts touches on another area of the fifth commandment, that is, the ways in which we might metaphorically kill another or ourselves. For example, we may drain others of life through our anger and resentment toward them, manifested in unkind words or actions. We may hold grudges that kill relationships and harm many others. We may even tell truths about others under the guise of honesty when it is really vengeance that lies in our hearts. Further, speaking and acting out of these death-dealing sentiments in our hearts "kill" not only the other but us too, as we harden our own hearts with sinful attitudes and actions. Jesus' reference to the fifth commandment reminds us to be careful not simply about what we say or do but also about what resides in our hearts. That, too, can damage and destroy our relationship with God and with others.

One could write books on what is forbidden by the fifth commandment and the various ways in which we literally and figuratively take life from others. However, our study of the commandments intends not simply to point to the boundaries beyond which we should not go nor simply to enlighten us regarding the limits to human freedom. It should also direct us to those virtues and actions that a lover of life ought to possess both for his or her own good and for the good of others.

One virtue closely associated with the fifth commandment is solidarity. Pope John Paul II described solidarity as "a firm and persevering determination to commit oneself to the common good; that is to say to the good of all and of each individual." Should we raise the question "Why?" he continues: "because we are all really responsible for all" (On Social Concern [*Sollicitudo Rei Socialis*], 38). Moving from what is forbidden to what we are called to by the fifth commandment, we may start with the virtue of solidarity. To live in solidarity with others is to have a heart and live a life that is caught up with concern for the common good, the good of others, so that they flourish as human beings.

A second virtue we could associate with the fifth commandment is justice. That is, in all we do, we should seek to harmonize our relationships with others and with God. Being a just person is not simply making sure that everyone gets an equal amount of what is distributed or that people receive what they have earned. It goes beyond these limited but reasonable notions of justice to a deep desire and committed action to right relationships with others so that they may flourish as human beings. Other virtues may also help us to live faithfully the spirit of the fifth commandment, but these two, solidarity and justice, will strengthen our sense of the evil of the unjust taking of human life and move us to actions that nurture life.

What might solidarity and justice call us to by way of positive attitudes and actions toward ourselves and others? The Catechism reminds us of our obligation to care for the souls of others so that, through our actions, we may not lead them to sin; it reminds us of the need to care for our health and, consequently, the health of others. It calls us to be respectful of persons in research and to avoid harm to the bodily integrity of a person. Again, one can imagine an almost endless list of ways in which we might act in solidarity and justice for the common good. Seeking health care for everyone would be a concrete example.

We might conclude, however, by recalling the scene in Matthew in which Jesus addresses the criteria for entrance into the kingdom. He divides the group based on their actions on behalf of or their failure to act on behalf of "the least of these who are members of my family" (25:40). Who are these? Identifying with them, Jesus says: "I was hungry and you gave me food, I was thirsty and you gave me something to drink, I was a stranger and you welcomed me, I was naked and you gave me clothing, I was sick and you took care of me, I was in prison and you visited me" (25:35–36).

Living the fifth commandment is surely about being vigilant about the unjust taking of human life; but it also calls us to virtues and actions that foster human life, especially in the case of the "least," who may die slow deaths because of other forms of injustice.

A specific example of the convergence of clarity about the evil of the unjust taking of human life and care for the living came to mind as I reflected on this commandment. In the United States, a Sunday in October is set aside as Respect Life Sunday. Ordinarily bishops of dioceses write a letter of some sort to the faithful to remind them precisely of the sacredness of human life.

In 1991 Bishop Kenneth Untener of Saginaw, Michigan, wrote a letter to the people of his diocese asking them to join him in making a commitment to help anyone who was confronting difficulties and might consider an abortion. Addressing these latter as "friends," he listed various situations they might be facing: fear of telling parents, pressure from another to abort a child, lack of access to prenatal care, insufficient funds to obtain medical services or to support another child, feelings of isolation, or family problems. In each instance, in one way or another, he wrote, "Let us know what you are struggling with and we'll help you." (See "Those Struggling with Abortion Decision," *Origins*, January 16, 1992.)

I met Bishop Untener nearly a year later and told him how impressed I was with his letter. He said that, to his knowledge, seventy-five people had approached the diocese for assistance because of that letter. The bishop and his diocese demonstrated justice and solidarity as described by John Paul II in a speech in 1979: "Solidarity means, above all, a proper understanding and then proper action... on the basis of the real needs of the person being helped, and what corresponds to his or her dignity."

The "why" for respecting human life from the womb to the tomb and for nurturing human life at all stages in between is so that others may live according to their dignity as children of God and one day share eternal life with God. Formed in solidarity and justice, we, as lovers of life, may be instrumental in helping others on their way to God and, in the process, pave our own way, with God's grace, to the kingdom.

■ ■ ■

Bringing Home the Message

Many people are raised with the belief that the Ten Commandments are black and white. They say what they mean and mean what they say. But over the years, we learn that there are times when things aren't as cut and dried as they appear to be. The fifth commandment bears this out as the author of this chapter early on draws a distinction: If your life is as sacred as mine, and my life is threatened, I can act in a way to preserve my life. This action might include taking someone's life. So we're presented with ambiguity on a topic that seems so obvious at first glance. Deeper reflection on this point calls for understanding the difference between the just and unjust taking of human life.

To live is to face decisions, and to move forward with life means taking risks when we decide on a course of action. Of these decisions, some will come back to haunt us because we have hurt ourselves or others. Seeing ourselves as moral agents is one of the profound lessons of this commandment, because to keep this commandment requires we examine our motives regarding how we treat others. Thus enter the values of justice and charity. How quickly we've moved from what seems an obvious prescription about taking life to uncovering the conditions necessary for human life to live with a degree of protection in order for it to prosper. Jesus spent a lot of time uncovering people's intentions, and the solid spiritual life maintains a healthy relationship between what one says and what one does.

The author writes, "Moving from what is forbidden to what we are called to by the fifth commandment, we may start with the virtue of solidarity. To live in solidarity with others is to have a heart and live a life that is caught up with concern for the common good, the good of others, so that they flourish as human beings." Why might this be true?

We are fragile creatures and sometimes respond in ways that take life and do not promote it. Understanding this connection is core to living the fifth commandment. Reflect on a time when you were wounded, not physically, but spiritually or psychologically. Are you able now, with some detachment, to see how the person who hurt you may have been acting out of pain? Why is it important to examine your motives before you respond in a cutting or cruel way? How might you change your verbal manners so that what you want to say gets communicated in a more constructive manner? What one topic surrounding the fifth commandment is most important to you after reading this chapter? Why?

6

You shall not commit adultery.

(*CCC* 2321-2400)

What God Has Joined, Let No One Separate: Living the Sixth Commandment

Dianne Bergant, CSA

Concern for family values becomes a heated topic for discussion in the United States around election time. Often the lifestyles of the candidates are meticulously scrutinized, since many voters maintain that a candidate who does not live according to such values will hardly be able to ensure that the community will. Two principal issues included under the heading of "family values" are the nature of marriage itself (Is it always permanent? Is it only between a woman and a man?) and the question of children (Is birth control allowed? If so, which forms? Though abortion is legal in this country, is it morally acceptable?). These questions, which flow from concern for family values, are some of the heated issues we face.

We talk about family values, but what are they? The commandment that sets the context for authentic family values is "Thou shalt not commit adultery." The Catechism identifies it as the sixth commandment. However, when counting the commands that constitute the biblical Decalogue (Exodus 20:1–17; Deuteronomy 5:6–21), some scholars identify it as the seventh commandment. Its place in the listing is not the point here.

At issue are the meaning and importance of the sixth commandment. What does it mean? The way most people understand this
commandment is from a contemporary point of view: What does
it mean to us today? However, if we examine the style in which this
command is written, we might uncover some very interesting insight
into its actual meaning. Finally, we can try to uncover the point of
view of the author and the community for which it was originally
meant. All three of these points of view will be examined here in
order to grasp the rich meaning of this directive.

WHAT DOES IT REALLY SAY?

The language of the commandment, "Thou shalt not...," is rather
archaic. Still it is the form that most people know. However, several
characteristics about this form should be noted. First, the Hebrew
pronoun thou is masculine singular in form. Does this mean that
the prohibition was only intended for men, as a strict literal reading might suggest? The answer to this question is yes and no. I will
explain this ambiguity in a moment. The negative form of the commandment has been understood by many as an example of the rigid
legalistic character of biblical law, particularly ancient Israelite law.
However, this is a misunderstanding of the way prohibitive directives
function. If we think about this for a moment, we will realize that
this kind of commandment is actually quite open. It simply states
the one form of behavior that is forbidden. It presumes implicitly
that other kinds of behavior are acceptable.

This particular commandment is really rather permissive when
it comes to sexual behavior. It does not suggest that sexual behavior
is ignoble. Ancient Israel was not prudish when it came to sexual
behavior. This particular commandment prohibits only one form of
behavior, adultery, which is described as illicit sexual activity between a
married person and someone other than that person's spouse. (Strictly

speaking, this commandment says nothing about fornication, which is illicit sexual behavior between unmarried individuals. However, traditional instruction has incorporated all directives regarding sexual behavior into the catechesis on this commandment.)

We must remember that the social structure of ancient Israel was patriarchal (father-headed). This explains why the form of the pronoun is masculine singular and why, on the one hand, we might say that the command was only intended for men. However, the head of a patriarchal household not only spoke for everyone in that household but also represented the entire household to the outside world. So in a sense, the commandment that was addressed to the male head of the household was intended for everyone in that household. But what did it really mean?

WHAT DID IT MEAN THEN?

In an ancient patriarchal society, the reproductive potential of a woman did not belong exclusively to her, as many believe is the case in our society today. That potential really belonged to the family and, in a broader sense, to the tribe. It was one of the means, in some ways the primary means, through which the people would survive in a world in which human life was constantly threatened. For the sake of the family and the tribe, this reproductive potential had to be guarded. This explains why women were normally confined to the interior of the home and were accompanied by a guardian whenever they went out in public. After all, the women carried within their bodies the greatest treasure of the family and the tribe, and that treasure had to be protected at all times. In such a culture, adultery was more than a sexual sin. It was a serious theft, a violation of the treasure of the entire tribe. More than this, it was a threat to its survival.

Adultery was committed whenever this treasure was violated. Therefore, a married woman was guilty of adultery whenever she had sexual relations with any man who was not her husband. Her sin was not only against her husband personally, but against her entire family or tribe, for her reproductive potential belonged to them. (Though the sinful wife of the prophet Hosea is described as a prostitute, her promiscuity was really participation in the Canaanite fertility cults. Thus her sexual behavior, which is metaphorically described as adultery, was really a form of idolatry or worship of a false god.) On the other hand, a man was guilty of adultery if he had sexual relations with someone else's wife. He sinned, not because he was unfaithful to his own wife, but because he violated the treasure of another man, or family, or tribe. This explains why a married man who visited a prostitute was not considered an adulterer.

This procreative potential of the woman was not valued for its own sake, but for the sake of the furtherance of the family into the next generation. Again, in this community-centered society, children were not valued merely for the sake of the children themselves, but for the sake of the continuance of the family into the next generation. This should not be seen as unjust manipulation of some within the society. Everyone—men, women, and children—served the fundamental goal of survival. In so doing, they developed respect for each member of the family as a vital contributing member as well as a remarkable sense of universal community loyalty.

These customs may appear to modern-day people to be strange and unfair to women and children. However, without justifying them, it is important that we understand them within their historical context so that we can better grasp the meaning intended by the commandment, "Thou shalt not commit adultery." In a certain sense, the ancient Israelites may well have had a much better understanding of the family values that lie behind this prohibition. For them, this commandment safeguarded the integrity of the present family, and it ensured that the family or tribe would survive into the future.

WHAT DOES IT MEAN NOW?

Today we live in an entirely different kind of society. While survival continues to be a serious problem for many people, international laws exist that prohibit the extinction of families, tribes, or entire nations. In many areas of life we have made great strides in dismantling gender bias. Furthermore, family is understood in many very different ways. Finally, a significant shift in perspective has taken place, particularly in the West, from a group-centered to an individual-centered consciousness. Changes such as these help to explain why adultery is now considered a breach in the bond that joins committed partners rather than a violation of the reproductive rights of the community. However, this shift in perspective does not nullify every aspect of the earlier understanding of this commandment. In many ways, the fundamental emphasis on family values remains.

In 1998 the Committee on Marriage and Family of the National Council of Catholic Bishops issued a tenth-anniversary document entitled "A Family Perspective in Church and Society" in which they provided the following definition of family: "A family is an intimate community of persons bound together by blood, marriage, or adoption, for the whole of life. In our Catholic tradition, the family proceeds from marriage—an intimate, exclusive, permanent, and faithful partnership of husband and wife." The contemporary reverence for the individual is evident in this statement. However, so is the community dimension that lies at the basis of the ancient perspective. The stated importance of marriage certainly refers to the bond between the woman and the man, but blood or adoption implies that there are children, and as was realized by the ancient Israelites, children are the promise of the family's future. While today we view adultery as a violation of the commitment between the married partners, we must be reminded that such infidelity threatens the stability of the entire family unit, not merely the married couple. All members of the family, adults and children alike, and the larger community as well need the stability that comes from fidelity in order to thrive. Furthermore, such fidelity acts as a model for children to emulate, thus ensuring family stability for the future.

The bishops' document discusses four elements that touch the heart of contemporary family life. The first is a Christian vision of family life in which the family places Christ at its center. Placing Christ at its center makes the family the first and basic domestic church. The second element views the family as a developing system of values. This means that the relationships between and among the family members change as members grow and mature or age and decline. The third element recognizes the diverse manifestations of family: nuclear family, extended family, single-parent family, and so forth. Finally, the family has relationships and responsibilities with other social institutions. As the important family values are nurtured they enable the members to interact appropriately with those outside of the family, thus spreading these values to the broader society. None of this would be possible if the members of the family could not depend upon the stability that fidelity assures them.

Using the characteristics of marriage as stated above, one might rephrase the commandment in the following positive way: "Thou shalt be intimate, exclusive, permanently committed, and faithful." These are the family values that will enable us all, adults and children, to grow in love and loyalty. They are the values that inspired some of the tenderest expressions of God's love for us: "I have loved you with an everlasting love" (Jeremiah 31:3); "No one has greater love than this, to lay down one's life for one's friends. You are my friends…" (John 15:13–14). This kind of love makes us like God, who loves us intimately, exclusively, permanently, and faithfully, and enables us to love others in this way.

■ ■ ■

Bringing Home the Message

Context shapes behavior and understanding. Learning that the Hebrew people were community-centered does give us a perspective on how this commandment worked to protect the tribe's survival. Identity through community, not individuality, is a shift for the contemporary reader. Even Burger King promises us that when we purchase food we can "Have it [our] way." The author of this chapter reminds us of the communal context for all the commandments and the need for individual behaviors to align with the needs of society. At moments when the community's collective identity was challenged by foreign powers or corrupt unfaithful leaders, the Decalogue, the Law, and the preaching of the prophets could remind the people of the relationship into which God invited them.

Bringing home the message today requires that believers retrieve the wisdom found in the past. Reading the "signs of the times" communicates the truth of that wisdom in a new era. A modern person from the West understands the sixth commandment to denounce adultery as a sin between two individuals. So how is this commandment relevant today? The following questions may help you understand how it still guides us in modern times.

What qualities are necessary for a person to be able to enter into and grow through a loving, committed relationship? Do you believe that a marriage, even though it might not be blessed by the Church, has a "sanctity," and that if that sanctity is not respected, it can harm people besides the spouses? Why is this so?

The author writes that this commandment might be recast in the following way: "Thou shalt be intimate, exclusive, permanently committed, and faithful." Explain in your own words how Christians make Christ present in a love that is "intimate, exclusive, permanent, and faithful." How does this commandment help you understand and explain the phrase "family values"?

7

You shall not steal.

(*CCC* 2401-2463)

Promoting a Community of Trust and Justice: Living the Seventh Commandment

Raphael Gallagher, C.Ss.R.

Crime stories about stealing fascinate us, from the big-time heist of The Great Train Robbery to the more mundane pilfering of the shoplifter in the mall. We know these things are wrong. But why? To understand the sense of the seventh commandment, we need to go back to the beginning of the story, long before the days of trains or malls.

When the Israelites were freed from Egypt, they took the risk of starting a new community based on shared values. Members agreed to live according to shared moral norms, believing that community was possible only if each took responsibility for the welfare of the others. A useful way of understanding the commandments is to see them as the promise of God's Word to the people of Israel in the form of a treaty, or covenant. On one side, God promises, "I will be your God, and you will be my people." The other side of the treaty explains what was expected of the people. If they wanted God's protection, they had to accept the conditions of the treaty, which are spelled out in the Ten Commandments.

Rather than laws imposed from the outside, the commandments are freely accepted conditions of a way of living. The first condition, of course, is that the Israelites accept that God is Lord of all. From that flow the other nine commandments. These explain, in detail, the type of moral behavior expected of individual Israelites. "You shall not steal" (Exodus 20:15; see also Deuteronomy 5:19) is a crucial part of the covenant agreement the commandments represent.

Scholars now generally agree that the original meaning of the commandment was to forbid kidnapping a person. The story of the sale of Joseph by his brothers, told in the Book of Genesis (see 37:12–36), was a reminder of the value of personal freedom. Only God is the Lord of life, and no one has the right to kidnap—or in other words steal—any person. With time, this interpretation took on a wider sense. Not only was kidnapping forbidden, but the unlawful taking of possessions necessary for life gradually came to be included as well.

The original meaning of the seventh commandment and its gradual extension to the necessities for preserving life explain the values that are at stake when we say "you shall not steal." Two values are central to understanding this commandment: trust and justice. These are necessary to guarantee the boundaries within which people can feel their lives are safe, not just from kidnapping but from anything that threatens the necessities of life. Safe homes and peaceful neighborhoods are built on a sense of trust. A just society is possible only when people, especially the poor, trust that they will have the opportunity to enjoy a decent standard of living.

Media reports and perhaps unfortunate personal experiences underline the need to recover these values in our society. Muggings and burglaries are too common. We could add to the list: being cheated in a business deal, being the victim of a pickpocket, or being conned by some shrewd insurance agent. Trust grows when people encounter trustworthy people; it diminishes when we live in constant fear of being robbed in any way. Maybe it was easier in the rural type of community in which the covenant of the commandments first existed, but the fact that it was necessary to stipulate even then that "you shall not steal" comes as a fair warning that the same commandment is even more valid in a society in which our neighborhoods are a mixture of strangers rather than friends.

The value of trust is meant to free people from the many forms of human greed. This greed can range from something as simple as stealing a soda from a chain store to insider trading on the stock exchange and includes everything in between, from charging a client for work not done to filing fraudulent tax returns. People sometimes feel they are being very smart in doing any of these things, but they are wrong, because these types of actions undermine the sense of trust, on which community is built.

The seventh commandment is also a call to respect the justice of God in the world. Here, I think, our sins against the seventh commandment are sins more of omission than of commission. We can do little immediately to uplift the lot of the poor: giving a dime may ease our conscience for a brief moment but usually solves nothing. What more could we do to be faithful to the values of the seventh commandment?

For one, I think we should be more active in social-justice issues, tackling the roots of problems in an unjust society that breeds a culture of stealing. Systematic injustice can be found in the practices of greedy businesses and unethical banks, in unfair health costs, and in educational policies that doom inner-city children to substandard education or perhaps even to illiteracy. We, as Catholics, have taken a too-narrow view of the seventh commandment in the past, justifying ourselves by saying, "Well, I didn't steal anything myself." But we are omitting something. What have we done to create a sense of community in which trust is nurtured and justice fostered? Not to steal is a negative commandment, relatively easy for most people to keep.

Promoting a community of trust and justice is more positive—and more difficult.

Talking of the original meaning of the seventh commandment, even outlining the values at stake, might seem rather abstract. Stealing is about the unlawful taking of others' property against their wishes. To know how to be faithful to this commandment, we need to understand the Christian attitude to property in its various forms.

Christians believe in the right to own private property. This is not because we are capitalists but because we are Christians. Owning goods is a legitimate condition in human life, provided we recognize that ultimately the world belongs to God. Ownership in the Christian sense does not imply the exclusive right of possession. That is what makes the Christian view of property different from the capitalist view. For capitalists, possession and ownership give a person the right to do whatever he or she likes. For Christians, just because we legally own something doesn't give us the right to use it however we wish.

The Christian justification of owning private property is fairly simple. We believe that ownership is a derived right, not a right inherent in the property itself. We are the trusted stewards of the created world. It is God who bestows the goods of the earth and determines their fruitfulness. Christians are entitled to own a reasonable amount of private property, provided, as I said, that we respect that limit. The greatest sin against the seventh commandment is when we literally steal the world from God's care and providence and treat it as if it were solely our own to do with as we please. Owning private property is legitimate, but it is given to us in trust for right use. There is no absolute right to own private property. That right is relative to our accepting that the goods of the earth are the Lord's, not ours.

Here we can glimpse a very contemporary relevance for the seventh commandment. Care for the environment, protection of natural resources, arranging for separate pickup of recyclable trash, supporting movements to decrease our emissions of carbon dioxide and chlorofluorocarbons: these ideas are not only for the politically correct; they are implied in a correct observance of the seventh commandment. This world is not for our generation only; it is meant by God for generations to come. When we destroy the environment—either in smaller ways such as thoughtless littering or in the more frightening ways of destroying limited natural resources—we are in fact stealing. We are taking for ourselves something that we do not own. The earth belongs to the Lord, and the Lord wants future generations to enjoy it and not have it destroyed by a greedy generation.

The seventh commandment implies personal and social obligations. What a difference it would make if we internalized these obligations. Instead of installing ever more sophisticated burglar-alarm systems, arming ourselves to the teeth, padlocking anything that moves, and living as if we expected to be robbed soon and often, we would trust people. I know that this may sound rather romantic, suggesting a return to an idyllic past (which never existed anyhow). I sense that in our Western society there are twin fears: social anarchy on the one hand and paranoid security arrangements on the other. "You shall not steal" is a commandment that avoids both extremes, because observing it would increase trust among people and build up social justice. Maybe that is a dream too, but it is the one the Israelites tried when they freely agreed to live in a certain way in order to have God's protection.

Modern society is more complex, of course. Stealing has become very sophisticated. Because copyright laws are difficult to enforce in this Internet age, we may be tempted to download and use material that does not belong to us as if it were, in fact, our private property. Insider trading may apply to only a wealthy few who can play the stock-market game, but it, too, is stealing information from others and pretending it is ours alone. The commandment not to steal applies to the older forms of petty pilfering as well as to new forms of sophisticated robbery based on the Internet. Living in this world as stewards of God's bounty in creation, maintaining a respect for private property but still showing a concern for the social needs of others, being honest in our business deals, and protecting a sustainable environment for tomorrow's generation: all of this is implied in the commandment "You shall not steal." If we truly kept the seventh commandment, how much more secure would be the protection of personal life, the original sense of the commandment?

The seventh commandment is a prohibition: "You shall not steal." It is tempting to get lost in the details: Was a particular act of stealing a serious or slight sin? Was stealing in certain circumstances justified? We would do better to concentrate on the vision that lies at the heart of the commandment. When we kidnap someone or take others' valid property against their wishes, we steal the precious gift of freedom. The commandments celebrate personal freedom; that is what is positive about the seventh commandment. In a sense, it is easy to keep the negative side of the commandment not to steal. Harder, although even more important, is to live by the vision on which it was founded. We acknowledge that God is our only true God when we respect the legitimate rights of stewardship of the earth that God asks us to live by.

It is debatable which of the Ten Commandments is the hardest to live by, but I would make a case for the seventh being the most difficult. In today's world, dominated by capitalist values, greed rules and possessions give power. We can become slaves to property and wealth almost without knowing it, and we can drift into subtle forms of stealing by engaging in activities such as fiscal evasion, corruption of public finances, or plagiarizing from the Internet. There is a crying need for rules to govern the capitalist world in which we live.

The Catholic view of the seventh commandment is based on a due respect for private property, but it is imbued with an even deeper value. Property is a relative right. The commandment does not give details of what constitutes stealing. Perhaps that, too, is a sign of how free God leaves us. God promises that the just person will be rewarded and leaves it to us to work out the details of justice in the circumstances of life.

The seventh commandment is a good guide as we conduct our personal dealings with property, and we have a long tradition on this point. But it is also a signpost to guide us in the complex world of capitalist values, in which there is little room for the meek and the mild. When we say "you shall not steal," we are not endorsing a passive attitude to today's complex world. On the contrary, we are saying that justice is integral to the value of freedom, the liberty of the person, and legitimately owned property. Only the strong are able to live by the commandment "You shall not steal."

■ ■ ■

Bringing Home the Message

When you began to read this chapter you probably didn't think the seventh commandment's original meaning had anything to do with kidnapping. "Stealing" is an obvious term and there's probably not much need to explain what it means, right? But as we've seen in earlier chapters, there's something more going on here. For the Hebrews, the protection of people and later the protection of those elements needed to live were necessary conditions for survival.

Refusing to steal is not enough. Men and women must actively work to create trust so as not to be always looking at others with suspicion or in fear of being robbed. Without trust, one lives in fear of one's neighbor. Without trust, people lock themselves behind emotional and spiritual barricades and can't emerge to establish bonds of love and significant friendship. *With* trust there comes freedom to act in the way of justice.

Trust and justice are cornerstones of a Christian identity, which in turn is grounded in the belief that all of creation is a gift to us. The world and what we create with the work of our minds and hands is on loan, so to speak. There is a tendency to believe that we can do anything we want with what we create, but faith informs us otherwise. Without this connection, "You shall not steal" becomes just a rule to live by. Our lives are impoverished, for we robbed this commandment of its ability to shape our identity.

In what ways does our society tell us it is *OK* to steal? Can you name a time or two in your life when you chose not to trust or act justly? What prevented you from doing so? The author of this chapter talks about owning private property. He writes, "We believe ownership is a derived right, not a right inherent in the property itself." Defend that statement. What is he saying?

8

You shall not bear false witness against your neighbor.

(*CCC* 2464-2513)

To Tell the Truth: Living the Eighth Commandment

Stephen Rehrauer, C.Ss.R.

The use of speech (and law) for both good and evil is a major theme that runs throughout the entire Bible. Words can serve truth or falsehood, light or darkness, life or death. Creation begins with a "word" spoken by God the Father, who is the source and guarantor of all truth. God's word of promise is spoken again and again to patriarchs and prophets, who in turn witness to its truth in word and deed. The revealed promise is fulfilled in the coming of Jesus the Christ. Jesus, the "Word of God," is the way, the truth, and the life (see John 14:6), who comes into the world to testify to the truth, overcome death, and offer us eternal life. His apostles and disciples are consecrated as witnesses to the truth of God's love and fidelity.

The devil is the father of lies, the one who deceives and sows chaos. In Genesis, the fall of humanity begins with false witness, as the serpent accuses God of having duplicitous and deceitful motives. (See 3:4–5.) The willingness of the first humans to believe and act on that false witness brings disaster and death. Satan appears again in the Book of Job when he slyly suggests that Job is not nearly as good as he appears to be. (See 1:9–11; 2:4–5.) He reappears in Revelation as the "accuser of our comrades," who "has been thrown down"

(12:10–12). In the Gospels, the Pharisees falsely accuse Jesus of being in league with Beelzebul, thereby showing themselves to be children of the devil. (See Matthew 12:24.) False witnesses arise at the trial of Jesus to accuse him. (See Mark 14:55–59.) Pontius Pilate, rather than hearing the truth and acting on it to work justice, cynically questions its practical worth when he has an angry mob to quiet and an emperor to serve. (See John 18:38.)

Witness to truth can be violated in many ways: by telling lies about others; by believing these lies and acting on them; by remaining silent and failing to speak the truth in defense of the falsely accused, thus challenging or correcting lies; by failing to challenge and correct those who are deceived about their own self-righteousness; and by revealing private and embarrassing truths about others that nobody else has a right or a need to know.

The divinely inspired authors of the Books of Exodus and Deuteronomy knew how easily and how effectively trust can be abused and manipulated by means of speech, and they knew the horrible injustices that result from such abuse. They were deeply concerned that the truth be told, defended, and lived among the people of Israel, because well-ordered life in community requires the ability to trust one another. But obeying the eighth commandment also serves a second and more important goal: it ensures the integrity, effectiveness, and goodness of the law itself.

Many references to testimony and witness in the Hebrew Scriptures refer to how the eighth commandment is to be understood and applied. (See Exodus 20:16; Leviticus 19:15–16; 24:20–24; Numbers 35:30; Deuteronomy 5:20; 17:6; 19:15–20; Proverbs 19:5, 9; 24:28; 25:18; Sirach 21:28.) These are concretely illustrated in the famous story of the chaste Susannah's rescue. (See Daniel 13.) No decision is to be made on the basis of one witness alone. God cares for and will bring justice for those who suffer false accusations. One who bears false witness is to be punished according to the law of retribution, receiving the same punishment he or she sought to have imposed on another.

False accusations of adultery, theft, or blasphemy; spreading rumors; or making comments that erode respect for parents or public leaders: all of these strike at the very purpose and heart of the law of God. They take the law of God, whose purpose is to serve the cause of justice in community life, and they pervert it, turning it into a tool of injustice. Those who accuse falsely use the law of God as a weapon with which to harm others. They do violence to those they accuse, to the entire community, and to the law of God itself.

People say things they aren't absolutely sure of for many different reasons. Sometimes we take shortcuts and accept too easily as true what others say to us, particularly when we like those who are speaking. At times we don't bother to do the hard work of finding out whether what they are telling us is true. We sometimes judge others, not on the basis of concrete evidence and reliable witness, but because we want something to be true. We may be tempted to harm the reputation of those who challenge our opinions and prejudices, because if we can point out a flaw in them, we feel justified in not listening to them even if they are telling the truth. We speak or remain silent because we fear others might think less of us. Ultimately, we bear false witness because it works. It serves our purposes.

Jesus came into the world to bear witness to a powerful truth. This world is not all there is. This life is not all there is. God exists, and God is faithful. God loves us. In Jesus, we are offered eternal life. Knowledge of eternal life reveals that everything in this world is relative in value, empty in itself, unable to satisfy the deepest longings of our hearts and minds or to give meaning to our existence. Jesus testifies to the truth that we are made for God, that God can be known by us, and that only in relationship with God will we find authentic happiness and fulfillment.

Our success and importance do not rest on how much we accumulate, how admired or important we are in the eyes of others, how high we rise in the pecking order of society, how much we accomplish and have to "show for ourselves" to others. Rather, our lives have worth in and of themselves as expressions of God's love. We are made in God's image, with an eternal destiny that goes far beyond any of those things that this world considers to be the important and defining criteria for who is better or worse, more or less successful. Jesus testifies to the fact that it profits us nothing to "gain the whole world" if in doing so we lose ourselves (Matthew 16:26).

Knowing this central and most important truth changes our wants, freeing us from the power of lies in a faithless, cynical world. A life dedicated to the truth used in service of love of God and neighbor frees us from the human motivations that tempt us to engage in slander, gossip, rash judgment, the perpetuation of false stereotypes, the spreading of rumors, the dissemination of misinformation. We have no need to destroy the reputation of others, to knock them from their pedestal, to gain esteem by taking it away from those who are liked and admired more, or to protect ourselves from the competition by discrediting or denigrating them. Knowledge of God as the source and guarantor of justice in truth frees us from the felt need to "justify ourselves," which inevitably leads us to use truth and justice as weapons to serve our own selfish vision and purpose rather than as the expression of love for God and neighbor.

The commandment says explicitly that we are not to bear false witness against our neighbor. But the teaching of Jesus in the parable of the Good Samaritan reveals its true spirit. (See Luke 10:25–37.) Living the commandment requires authentically worshiping God in spirit by loving our neighbors. Speaking only the truth about them and to them is a tangible way of loving.

Neighbors are defined as the ones against whom we do not bear false witness, those in whose defense we speak by telling only the truth that we know with certainty, which we speak only for their benefit. Concern for the truth transforms others into our neighbors; when we speak only the truth about and to others, they become our neighbors. When we bear false witness against others, we are in fact engaging in violence against them, transforming them into our enemies. Called as Christians to love our neighbors, when we tell a falsehood about or to them, we distort our own Christian identity.

The disciple of Christ is consecrated to bear witness to truth. (See John 17:17.) To bear witness is first and foremost to communicate what we know. We can know things in several ways: by our own experience and by way of what we have been told by others in whom we place our trust. To be authentic and credible witnesses to Christ requires that we know him and actually believe the truth he teaches. It also requires that our actions be coherent with the truths we believe. To bear effective witness to the truth, we must be truthful people whose lives are centered on seeking first the kingdom of God.

We need to take great care before speaking and judge very carefully what others say to us. In a world of lies, we must be wise as serpents and gentle as doves, quick to listen, slow to speak. This becomes the test of the true believer, the authentic witness. The authentic witness carefully examines what is heard, is able to distinguish the truth from the lie, and speaks only the truth. In bearing true witness about others, we also bear authentic witness to others. We are not only credible in the eyes of others; we are also worthy of their trust. The positive call of the commandment takes tangible form. We are commanded to transform all people into our neighbors by bearing true witness to Christ's love.

When we respect the truth and speak only the truth about one another as an expression of love for God and neighbor, living the commandment becomes an act of worship and a blessing. When we love others as God loves them, we discover the power of God's grace in our lives—a power that enables us to rise above and beyond our own human pettiness and shortsightedness and overcome our fears, allowing us to do great things with and for one another. We enter the kingdom of light and truth. Christ gives us the courage and the wisdom to know what to say and when so that the truth we speak will serve only goodness. We witness the power of God to change the lives of people here and now, and we witness to this power. We find that God has given us the power to live the Christian version of the eighth commandment described by Saint Paul. We say "only what is useful for building up, as there is need, so that [our] words may give grace to those who hear" (Ephesians 4:29).

Those who worship God must do so in spirit and in truth. All law and prophecy can be summarized in two points: love God, and love your neighbor. The eighth commandment speaks to our hearts as followers of Christ, calling us as the Christian community to authentic worship of God by defending, speaking, and living the truth about our neighbors—a truth that is a loving witness of good news and hope for a world otherwise condemned to live in suspicion, doubt, uncertainty, chaos, and confusion. We seek and know the truth, and we discover that the truth has set us free.

■ ■ ■

Bringing Home the Message

Each year on Good Friday, we hear John's account of Jesus' passion. Pilate asks Jesus a question during his interrogation: "What is truth?" (John 18:38). Pilate had a decision to make about Jesus and his future, and he knew his decision could help or hurt his own career. What was the truth? The author of this chapter, a moral theologian, says, "A life dedicated to the truth used in service of love of God and neighbor frees us from the human motivations that tempt us to engage in slander, gossip, rash judgment, the perpetuation of false stereotypes, the spreading of rumors, the dissemination of misinformation." How might this lifestyle play out in our everyday lives? Give an example.

The obligation to act on what we know to be true carries a great responsibility for each and every adult. There are times when we can shade the truth or hide a fact, but we know better. We know that we failed in living life fully. This fullness means that we live for a good that goes beyond self interest or self fulfillment. We live a full life when we learn to overcome the stereotypes that form our judgments, and when we learn to make friends out of strangers. We live a full life when we take an unpopular stand, promoting the dignity of the poor and others who are trampled by the self-righteous.

To live this way requires courage and humility. We must admit we don't have all the answers to the dilemmas that confront us, and we need to listen to those who have something to offer. It takes courage to pursue the truth, even when the answer—and its pursuit—are unpopular. To not "bear false witness" brings to the forefront the fact that Christians do live for a purpose that many people don't understand. It brings a reward that won't always increase what we have in the bank. We are thus freed to live for others and not tell lies about them, to live in ways that promote others' dignity.

How would you explain the power of words to take life or give life? When have you lived with the freedom that comes in knowing that God offers you a life that will never end? What are some of the "fruits" of living this commandment well?

9

**You shall not covet
your neighbor's wife.**

(CCC 2514-2533)

10

**You shall not covet
anything that is
your neighbor's.**

(CCC 2534-2557)

Thou Shalt Not Be Unhappy: Living the Ninth and Tenth Commandments

Paul Wadell, PhD

We are seekers of happiness, pilgrims searching for bliss. And God's commandments are our most trustworthy guides. But wait a minute. Don't we normally think more commandments mean less happiness and fewer commandments mean more happiness? Don't we picture laws and commands as hindrances to happiness, not pathways to happiness? But God commands us to do all kinds of things and to refrain from doing other things—not to frustrate us, but to show us how to be good at being human. Everyone wants to be happy, but happiness is something we learn and grow into as we discover what is truly good for us. The Ten Commandments tutor us in the ways of happiness by moving us toward God, our most excellent and exquisite good, and by teaching us how rightly to seek and to love everything else in light of God. They help us take our first feeble steps in the ways of happiness by delineating what frustrates and threatens happiness, as well as what protects it.

The ninth and tenth commandments call our attention to mistaken paths to happiness. Rather earthy and straightforward—and perhaps embarrassingly honest—they remind us that we will not find bliss by feverishly coveting things that do not belong to us, whether a neighbor's spouse, wealth and material possessions, "or anything that belongs to [our] neighbor" (Exodus 20:17). Do we really need to be reminded of actions that we know, if pursued, can only end badly? Did God have to be so forthright about the more sordid possibilities of human behavior?

These commandments testify that the God who created us knows us—as well as some of our more wayward inclinations—better than we know ourselves. We may be seekers of happiness, but we are also seekers who commonly go astray. We are mixed-up lovers who cannot help but pursue what we think will be good for us but who are renowned for being confounded and confused about what that good might be. Like Saint Augustine, whose famous prayer guarantees that our hearts will be restless until they rest in God, we can spend a good bit of our lives casting about for things to love, while feeling increasingly depleted for our misguided attempts.

The ninth and tenth commandments are all about desires, particularly what to desire and how to desire. They deal with the power of desires at work in our hearts and warn us to be careful. They recognize that desires are part of our nature. But they also remind us that misguided desires can not only dominate and control us but can harm us—and others—in ways we often only belatedly discover. We cannot live without desires and longings. But we have to be honest about what we desire and how we desire, because our desires shape our character and direct our lives. If we are not to end up strangers to happiness, we need to heed what these last two commandments can teach us about learning to desire good things in the right way.

The Ninth Commandment

"You shall not covet your neighbor's wife" (Exodus 20:17). Sounds almost quaint, doesn't it? Especially in a culture in which we are trained to be coveting creatures, men and women who, no matter what we have, are convinced that all our troubles will vanish if we only have this one thing more, even if it's another person's spouse. Films and television shows today are awash with conniving individuals lusting after somebody's spouse, so much so that we feel something is wrong with us if we, too, have not set our sights on obtaining what belongs to another. And accompanied by a laugh track, the coveting of another's husband or wife seems not only inevitable but also benign, even healthy. It's as if we've been taught to expect lies, deceit, and betrayal more than faithfulness, as if there's something wrong with us not when we break the vows and promises of our lives, but when we keep them. Contrary to the ninth commandment, a society that has trained us to put our own needs and desires over the well-being of others, including the persons we've promised to love, teaches that the path to happiness is found not in faithful love, but in novelty and titillation. In this respect, coveting another's spouse is no different than coveting a new house or a new car. In each case the message is the same: the new is always better.

But the ninth commandment warns that taking such silliness to heart leads not to liberation, but to immense sadness and destruction. And the reason is that there is a crucial difference between fantasy and real love. Coveting is rooted in dissatisfaction and discontent. When we are restless and dissatisfied, we turn our sights to things we do not have that we are convinced will fill the emptiness of our lives. We daydream and we fantasize. We imagine lives (and spouses) quite different than the ones we have. We allow fantasies to transport us out of our real lives and into relationships where we are relieved of the hard work of real love. In the mists of reverie and daydreaming, affairs appear inviting, betrayals trifling, and love quite literally a day at the beach (as the sun sets and wine is sipped). Gone is the hard work of real love, parsed in practices of forgiveness, patience, tolerance, and good humor.

The danger of surrendering to such fantasies is not only that we use them to escape the real work of love but also that we begin to entertain temptations, eventually seeing them not as sins to avoid, but as plausible, inviting possibilities. Through fantasy we nurture desires we should avoid and picture ourselves in relationships and situations that, far from assuring the happiness we imagine, can only end badly. In this respect, the ninth commandment bids us to know ourselves well and to be honest about some of the misguided stirrings of our hearts. It counsels us to be alert to the dangers of unhealthy curiosity and to reflect on where our daydreams and musings take us. Do they take us out of our commitments or root us more deeply in them? Do they help us see our spouses, families, friends, and communities more graciously and compassionately, or do they lure us away from them in ways that render us both deceived and unfaithful?

Counting the Costs of Coveting

When we are restless and dissatisfied, instead of seeking refuge in fantasy, we should probe our discontent to discern what is missing in our lives and what will really bring us peace. Instead of fleeing our lives through endless daydreaming, we should embrace them more completely, including their challenges and limitations. And we should not be afraid to ask some potentially difficult questions: Do we need a better relationship with God? Do we need to be more aware of, and honest about, our own shortcomings and imperfections instead of being experts in the shortcomings of those we've promised to love? Do we need, as the psalmist writes, "a contrite heart" and a repentant spirit? How are we, in the loves of our lives, called to a deeper imitation of Christ?

Unless we wrestle with these questions, the lure of fantasy can blind us to the costs of covetous desires. Put more strongly, this commandment forbids coveting another's husband or wife precisely because acting on such a desire—no matter what we tell ourselves— leads to harm that is not easily undone. Indeed, covetous desires require self-deception, because we could hardly entertain them if we had any clue to the damage that will result if we act on them. For instance, if my attention is riveted on another's husband or wife, I will be tragically unmindful of all I risk losing (and destroying) if I abandon what was meant to be a lifelong commitment for the sake of something that is little more than a self-absorbed daydream. Caught in a web of deception, I will not see all I am about to throw away in exchange for something unreal. I will overlook the pain and sorrow that my actions will bring to others because my only concern will be the consolation I envision for myself. Most of all, I will no longer see the face of the one I vowed to love because in betraying him or her, I rivet my attention on one who belongs not to me, but to someone else.

This is why the ninth commandment (as well as the tenth) is really about justice. Justice governs our relationships with others, ensuring that we respect them, treat them fairly, and give them their due. To covet another's spouse is an egregious failure of justice in four respects. First, it violates the promise we made when we vowed to be faithful to another and told that person that he or she could take our words to heart; it makes that promise a lie. Second, it is unjust to the husband or wife to whom we promised our wholehearted love, presence, and attention because it makes a fantasy, and not our spouse, the center of our lives. Third, it is unjust to the spouse of the person we are coveting because, even if only in our imaginations, we are contemplating stealing what rightfully belongs to another.

And fourth, it is unjust to the person we are coveting because we are looking at that individual only as an object for our pleasure and not as someone who has dignity and sacredness as a child of God and thus deserves our respect.

The Tenth Commandment

"You shall not covet your neighbor's house…or male or female slave, or ox, or donkey, or anything that belongs to your neighbor" (Exodus 20:17). The things we covet today may be different—fancy cars, designer clothes, or our neighbor's swimming pool—but like our biblical ancestors, we know what it is to envy others for what they have and we lack. Besides, we live in a consumerist society whose favorite mantra is "I see it, I want it, I have to have it!" The tenth commandment is especially designed for a society such as ours, one that says we need things more than we need people and teaches us to measure success not by the richness of our loves, but by the accumulation of our possessions. The gospel of consumerism encourages us not, as Jesus counseled, to sell what we have and give the proceeds to the poor (Matthew 19:21), but to cling tightly to what we own and to crave what we do not yet have. Consumerism encourages us to be restless and dissatisfied so that we will always want more and buy more.

But what kind of person does this make us? What happens to us if we cultivate greed instead of generosity? The tenth commandment warns us of the dangers of greed and envy because such vices weaken our relationships with others, lead to discord and division, and foster attachments that will ultimately disappoint us. For example, if I am consumed with envy for what my neighbor has, I will hardly be able to appreciate what I have, including the important things in life such as good friendships, time for solitude and prayer, and even simplicity of life.

It is no wonder that in the Gospels, Jesus frequently warns of the dangers of wealth and the temptation to find our happiness and security in it. Such strategies for bliss always backfire because God made us to find joy, not in a mountain of possessions, but in love and communion with others. Greed, envy, and resentment work against the very things we need for happiness because they destroy the peace and fellowship that make true community possible. As Saint John Chrysostom wrote, when envy for another's possessions takes hold of us, "we devour one another like beasts" (as quoted in *Catechism of the Catholic Church*, 2538). Anyone who has watched sisters and brothers fight over what they will inherit from their parents knows how true this can be.

Envy and resentment never deliver the satisfaction we think they will; indeed, they fail us in all sorts of ways. If we spend our time envying our neighbors for what they have and we do not, we will never get to know them as the persons they are, much less develop friendships with them. We will never discover the freedom and joy that come from realizing life is a gift and that real and lasting happiness is found not in hoarding possessions, but in sharing them. As theologian Brian Johnstone has said, receiving and giving lie at the very core of our being. And this means we find life not by envying others for what they have, but by becoming "gifted givers" who are grateful for what we have and eager to share it with others.

COMING FULL CIRCLE

These last two commandments return us to the first because they remind us that if we love God most of all, we will know rightly how to love and cherish everything else. That is why, like all the commandments, these final two are trustworthy guides in our quest for happiness.

Bringing Home the Message

When we need to accomplish a task we sometimes ask, "What is our goal?" We start with what we hope to do and work backwards, filling in the steps necessary to reach the goal. If our desire is to be happy, then what are the necessary steps to achieve happiness? The author of this chapter writes, "We may be seekers of happiness, but we are also seekers who commonly go astray." With multiple desires at work, the odds for making poor decisions increase greatly. The directness of the last two commandments about coveting another's spouse or goods brings the message through our front door and into the personal areas of our lives. Getting a little uncomfortable?

To advance to the heart of these commandments requires some introspection. It may even include taking a personal inventory of the false loves we've pursued. Bombarded by messages from a consumerist society, we can easily lose core values, only to find them unthinkingly replaced with choices that reinforce our needs and ignore the higher moral principles such as respect of another's dignity. The next step is to rationalize the new, ill behaviors that have become habits. And down the slippery slope we go. . .

Believing we are owed a certain lifestyle leads us to compare ourselves to our neighbors. Feelings of envy arise, and a desire to live for ourselves evolves into the desire to pursue more goods. The power to purchase and provide for others becomes corrupted, and the communion that might grow is now choked by the weeds of isolation and self-preservation.

What does becoming a mature person have to do with discerning what brings true and false happiness? What gives rise to dissatisfaction and discontent in our lives? In a culture that equates self-worth with owning things, the Gospel has a powerful message of letting go and learning to give. In that light, ask yourself: Do I possess the kingdom of God, or does the kingdom of God possess me?

Conclusion

What more can be said after reading these chapters? A reader might note how often the theme of justice emerges, although it is not directly mentioned in any one of the chapter titles. The Decalogue points toward justice (Keep the Lord's name holy; Honor thy father and mother) and lays a moral foundation (Thou shalt not kill, lie, or covet). Like a succinct set of business principles, the Ten Commandments can guide personal and communal behaviors that promote human dignity. Bridging the centuries—from the time the commandments were incorporated into the Jewish Scripture through their incorporation into the Christian Tradition—is partly the work of theologians and partly the work of committed Christians. The wisdom of the Ten Commandments is effective when the men and women who live this wisdom engage their own questions about the meaning of life and are prepared to give words of hope and understanding to others. These commandments make possible the real and lasting connections we have with one another, even when we do not know each other personally. They make community possible.

In a world that depends on the accuracy of atomic clocks, the Ten Commandments might seem as effective as a sundial. However, while our culture seems even more lonely despite access to phones, email, and instant messaging, the Ten Commandments do connect men and women to God, the giver of life and all that is good. In a few years, computers and cell phones will be replaced with newer technology. Christians, meanwhile, can remain connected to the one source of joy and peace day in and day out—with no long distance charges.

Acknowledgments

"Swept Up by Love: Living the First Commandment" was previously published in *Liguorian*, May/June 2007. Copyright © 2007 Kevin J. O'Neil, C.Ss.R.

"Living Up to the Name of God: The Second Commandment" was previously published in *Liguorian*, September 2007. Copyright © 2007 Stephen T. Rehrauer, C.Ss.R.

"Rest, Worship, and Community: Living the Third Commandment" was previously published in *Liguorian*, December 2007. Copyright © 2007 Timothy E. O'Connell, PhD.

"Fathers and Mothers, Sons and Daughters: Living the Fourth Commandment" was previously published in *Liguorian*, February 2008. Copyright © 2008 Mara Kelly-Zukowski, PhD.

"Respect for Life: Living the Fifth Commandment" was previously published in *Liguorian*, March 2008. Copyright © 2008 Kevin J. O'Neil, C.Ss.R.

"What God Has Joined, Let No One Separate: Living the Sixth Commandment" was previously published in *Liguorian*, April 2008. Copyright © 2008 Dianne Bergant, CSA.

"Promoting a Community of Trust and Justice: Living the Seventh Commandment" was previously published in *Liguorian*, September 2008. Copyright © 2008 Raphael Gallagher, C.Ss.R.

"To Tell the Truth: Living the Eighth Commandment" was previously published in *Liguorian*, October 2008. Copyright © 2008 Stephen Rehrauer, C.Ss.R.

"Thou Shalt Not Be Unhappy: Living the Ninth and Tenth Commandments" was previously published in *Liguorian*, November 2008. Copyright © 2008 Paul Wadell, PhD.